DATE DUE		
OCT 19 2003	APR 14 2008	
JUL 2007	APR 15 2009	
JUL 12 2011	OCT 25 2012	

My Sahara Adventure

52 Days by Camel

by Lawrie Raskin with Debora Pearson

Photography by Lawrie Raskin

Annick Press • Toronto • New York

ACKNOWLEDGEMENTS

With so many thanks to so many people who shaped the direction of my life and helped make this book possible:

• To my older cousin Larry Lederman, who gave me his boxes of treasured comic books when I was a kid.

• To my parents, Al and Shirley, who gave me my love of books and reading; who had the foresight and courage to send their teenage son on his first travel adventure, an ocean freighter voyage to Europe; and who never threw out those old comics.

• To T.E. Lawrence ("of Arabia"), whose achievements and writings taught me that one *can* live one's dreams; and to Sir David Lean, whose vision created the cinema masterpiece that fired my imagination and led me to the desert.

• To my oldest friend, Barry Weinstock, who shared the excitement of my first venture into Africa; and to Armin Rigert, a Swiss traveller, with whom I first experienced the real desert.

• To the many warm and wonderful Moroccans, Mauritanians and Malians who opened their doors and my mind in the early days of my travels—particularly Tayour Mahjoub, artist and poet, Najmi Mohammed, a saint among men, Lamadar Latif, who taught me how to swear in Arabic, and Mir Boumedien, may he rest in peace.

• To Philip and Kinza Schuyler, Sam Lieberman, "Evil Jeff" Reinhart and Lance Lindabury, Americans living in Morocco, who shared their love and knowledge of the country and influenced me more than they'll ever know.

• To Abderrahman of Mhamid, who organized my first camel trip; and to Booba and Boomba, our trusty guides.

• To Mohammed Ould Mouloud Ould Daddah, in Nouakchott, who immediately knew my heart and helped me reach the difficult Mauritanian interior; and to Bokara and Sherif, for letting me share their lives when I got there.

• To Paul Bowles, American writer and resident of Morocco for half a century, for the power and beauty of his insightful work, and for his gracious hospitality.

• To Tony Dalton, explorer extraordinaire, with whom I managed to reach the salt mines at Taoudenni, one of the most remote desert destinations on Earth; to Bob Clark, who helped make that expedition possible; and to Moulay of Timbuktu, our gifted guide who, across hundreds of miles of featureless terrain, actually got us there.

• To Rick Wilks, my publisher, who conceived the brilliant idea of opening kids' eyes to the adventures this world has to offer.

• To Debora Pearson, my writer and editor, who did a truly heroic job in massaging dozens of hours of rambling, taped stories into this organized tale, while embarking upon her own adventure of new motherhood.

• To Sheryl Shapiro, designer, who somehow juggled tens of thousands of words, and sat through hundreds of my slides, in order to create the fine look of this volume.

• To Farida Zaman, illustrator, who endured my quest for accuracy in her production of the colourful route map.

This labour of love is dedicated to my sons Jamie and Josh, who, on several trips, have reminded me of just what things are really important in childhood, and who have given me the excuse, at times, to relive my own. I hope they will continue to explore and document this wide, wonderful world themselves.

And to Clara Marvin, my life partner and fellow adventurer, who to my never-ending wonder and amazement puts up with the chaos that always seems to accompany my projects.

Lawrie Raskin
Hotel Riad Salam
(52 days by camel from Timbuktu)
Zagora, Morocco

Many thanks to Lawrie Raskin for generously sharing his trip memories with me and teaching me almost everything I know about life in the Sahara, and to Sheryl Shapiro for her thoughtful and inspired design work, always executed with great care and unfailing good humour. Thanks also to Farida Zaman for her terrific map and assistance in fact-checking the Moslem and cultural information, and to Professor James Donaldson, Department of Chemistry, University of Toronto, for fact-checking the mirage text. And finally, a special word of thanks to Rick Wilks, Annick Press, who invited me on the astonishing adventure of creating this book, allowed me to wander with great freedom, and always trusted I would reach our destination.

For Michael and Benjamin, always with me on my adventures.

Debora Pearson
Toronto

How I Became a Desert Explorer

Ever since I was a kid growing up in Toronto, I wanted to see the desert. I'm an adult now, but I can still remember the first time I thought about taking a desert adventure. I had read a comic book in which Donald Duck and his nephews went to the Sahara, rode camels over sand dunes, and visited an oasis. I was so fascinated with this story that I read that comic over and over until it fell apart!

Later on, when I was a teenager, I saw a movie that made me want to go to the desert even more. The movie was *Lawrence of Arabia*, and I couldn't get enough of the scenes that were shot in the actual desert. I saw *Lawrence of Arabia* again and again, and it had the same effect on me as reading the comic book had years before, only stronger. I absolutely *had* to see a desert for myself. And so, several years later, I travelled to Africa to see the Sahara, the world's largest desert.

Some people who go to a place for the first time have a feeling that they've been there before. For me, that place is the Sahara. On my first trip there I felt like I belonged, almost like I had returned to my real home. I wanted to explore everything there, from the things that seemed strangely familiar to the things that seemed just plain strange.

Since my first trip there, I've explored the Sahara many more times. Going "home" all those times has changed my life and turned me into a desert expert. I've learned how to speak Arabic, lived with desert peoples, and organized many expeditions through the Sahara. I've discovered lots about life in the desert, but there will always be much more for me to learn – that's why I'll keep going back as often as I can. On each trip, I get excited all over again!

Exploring the desert has been – and is – the best adventure of my life. I hope that as you take this trip with me you'll feel some of the excitement I've felt. And who knows? Perhaps you'll start to think about some great adventures *you* can take, too!

Laurie Raskin

52 Days by Camel

I had seen the inside of a desert nomad's tent, viewed the Sahara while riding a camel, and eyed a desert scorpion up close, but this was the strangest sight I'd seen in Africa. I was looking at a road sign to Timbuktu!

Travelling to the Sahara had been a dream come true for me. But I had never imagined that I could also go to Timbuktu, an ancient, mysterious city far across the desert to the south. As a boy, I had heard the name "Timbuktu". It sounded like the most faraway place on Earth and I didn't even know if it was real.

Hundreds of years ago, Timbuktu had been an important destination for camel caravans and a place where gold, salt, and slaves were traded. Few outsiders had ever seen this city and, over time, the word "Timbuktu" came to stand for a place so far away that it seemed unreal. Yet here was a road sign that pointed the way to Timbuktu and gave the distance: 52 days. That meant 52 days by camel.

As I touched the sign again and again, I made up my mind. I was going to Timbuktu. I had to see it, smell it, explore it for myself. First, I had to find a way to get there. The sign pointed to an old caravan route that crossed the hottest, driest part of the Sahara. These days, almost all the camel caravans in Africa were gone and no one used this route any more. There were land mines along the way, left from past wars, and fiercely protected borders. How would I get there?

Here is the story of my amazing African adventure and how I finally got to Timbuktu…

This road sign in Arabic and French points to the mysterious, "lost" city of Timbuktu.

CHAPTER 1

Fun Times in Fez

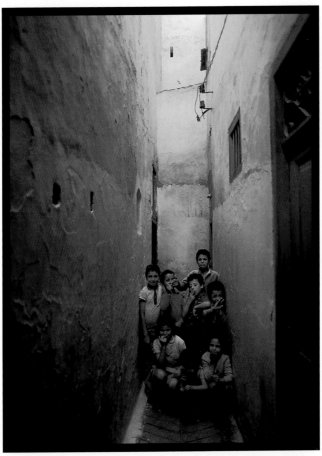

**A skinny street in Fez is a cool place to visit.
The tall buildings block out the blazing sun.**

Balek! Balek!" cried the old man in Arabic. "Get out of the way! Get out of the way!"

I turned around to see his donkey, weighed down with heavy baskets, about to run into me. In the nick of time, I jumped to the side of the narrow street and felt the donkey's load smash against my hips as it squeezed past. Yow! Now that really hurt!

Here, in the city of Fez, pedestrians didn't have to worry about being hit by cars. The streets, built centuries before the invention of cars, were too narrow, bumpy, and hilly for motor vehicles to travel on. But there were other dangers, such as donkeys, that I was becoming painfully aware of.

This giant "beehive" is really a tannery in Fez. It's where animal skins are turned into leather.

The old streets of Fez are too narrow for cars and trucks to drive on, so donkeys are often used instead, to carry heavy goods around.

Like Tangier, the only other city I had seen since arriving in Africa, Fez was strange and fascinating. I wanted to come here because Fez was famous for its carpets, silver work, and leather work. Long ago, it had been a stop along the camel caravan routes, a place where traders exchanged the goods they brought from the south for the beautiful items made in Fez. I liked the fact that Fez was an ancient city with walls around it and giant wooden gates that still swung shut each night, just as they had for centuries. Most parts of Fez hadn't changed in over a thousand years – as I looked at the shop signs in Arabic, smelled the spices in the market, and listened to the drummers by the gates, I felt as if I'd travelled back in time several centuries and was in Fez as it existed back then.

Even getting lost in Fez was part of my adventure. That's when I learned something amazing about the city. Like the houses in other North African cities, the traditional, old houses of Fez don't have bathtubs, showers, or ovens. Instead, when people

The Secret Past Life of Spices

It's hard to say what I liked most about the spices. Was it their bright colours, or rich aromas? Or was it the fact that spices had travelled with the camel caravans long ago?

need to bathe, they go with others to the public baths located in each neighbourhood. To bake bread, cakes, or pastries, the women of each house prepare the dough at home. It is then carried to the neighbourhood's central bakery, expertly baked in the ovens there, and brought back home and enjoyed fresh. Bakeries and baths are important.

As I wandered around the maze of streets, looking at the mosques and searching for my hotel, I gradually noticed something strange – I never saw a public bath building on the same street as a bakery.

When I asked a shopkeeper about this, he cleared up the mystery for me. Both baths and bakeries need fires, the baths to heat the water and the bakeries to heat the ovens. Instead of having separate fires, which take a lot of fuel and effort to maintain, the bath and bakery in each neighbourhood were built back-to-back so they could share the same fire. That's why you'll never see them together on the same street in Moslem cities, even though they are joined together!

Getting lost in Fez wasn't the only unexpected thing that happened to me. I also met

A Handy Way to Eat

"Don't eat with your hands!" "Don't get the table dirty!" In Morocco, kids never hear adults say any of these things. Why? Because eating with your hands and putting bones and other food bits on the table are what everyone does during a traditional Moroccan meal.

Before the meal begins, everyone washes their hands at the table using a pitcher of water, soap, and a towel. The food is served in one big bowl or platter that everyone can reach from where they sit. There are no knives, forks, spoons,

or plates to use. Instead, each person uses their right hand (never their left hand) to help themselves to the food facing them. (In Arab countries such as Morocco, the left hand is considered "unclean" because it's the hand people use for cleaning themselves after going to the bathroom.) People who really know how to eat Moroccan-style use just the thumb and first two fingers of their right hand to pick up pieces of their food.

Sometimes, at the end of the meal, the table is cleared by pulling together the corners of the tablecloth, with the serving dish and food "garbage" still on it, and whisking it away. No one ever gets stuck with washing lots of dishes after the meal – because the food is cooked in and eaten from the same dish, it's the only thing that needs to be cleaned!

---

a fellow traveller, a Swiss guy named Armin, who was driving a beat-up old van. He was a world traveller but he had never been to the desert. When I told Armin that I had come to Africa because I wanted to see the Sahara, he said something that surprised and delighted me: "I'm going south and would like to see the desert, too. You can come with me if you like."

That was all I needed to hear. I thanked Armin and told him that I accepted his offer. We made plans to leave Fez and start our journey south a few days later.

This English sign is for travellers who need to exchange money. Can you tell what it says?

What's a Mosque?

A mosque is the place of worship for believers of Islam, who are known as Moslems. All cities and towns in North Africa have at least one of these buildings, and you can judge the size of a city or town by the number of mosques it has – the larger the city, the more mosques you'll see.

How can you spot a mosque? Each one has a minaret, a tower topped by an ornament pointing up to the sky. This is the place where one person, known as a muezzin, calls Moslems to prayer five times each day. In places with many mosques, you'll often hear each call to prayer in something almost like stereo sound, as muezzins in all the mosques around you chant at the same time, forming overlapping ripples and echoes of the same sounds. This chanting is so eerie and haunting that you might feel chills running up and down your spine when you hear it.

You'll notice shoes piled outside the entrance to a mosque, too. Moslems remove their shoes before entering a mosque as a sign of respect for Allah, or God. Every Friday, when there is a special worship time in most larger mosques, there will be many pairs of shoes outside the mosque – a sure sign that many people have gathered inside.

Unlike other places of worship, such as churches and synagogues, mosques don't have seats for people to sit on. Instead, people stand or kneel on prayer mats that are laid out in a large, open space inside the mosque. When Moslems pray, they must face Mecca, the holy city of Islam, in Saudi Arabia. A hollow in the wall of every mosque, called a mihrab, shows worshippers the correct direction to face.

This mosque in Mali has a football-sized ostrich egg on top of each minaret.

What Does It Mean to Be a Moslem?

To be a Moslem, you must follow the religion of Islam. The word "Islam" means "submission or obedience to God" and is based on the belief in one God, named "Allah" in Arabic. Moslems, who live all over the world, believe that Allah sent a message to people over a thousand years ago in Arabia. This message was revealed to a prophet named Mohammed. Followers of Islam believe that the Koran, the Moslem holy book, is the actual words of God which Mohammed memorized and recited to his followers, and which were later written down.

Kids who are raised as Moslems grow up reading, memorizing, and reciting sections of the Koran. Like all Moslems, they are expected to treat the Koran with respect and follow the many rules that are found in it. These rules apply not only to the way Moslems worship and pray but also to the way they dress, what they eat and drink, and how they act.

Every Moslem has certain duties to perform which are called "The Five Pillars of Islam". The five pillars are praying (which is done five times daily), affirming or declaring one's faith, fasting once a year, giving alms to help less fortunate Moslems, and making a pilgrimage to Mecca, the holy city of Islam, in Saudi Arabia.

Snow in hot, sunny Africa? That's exactly what
I saw as we drove closer and closer to the Atlas
Mountains, on our way south to the Sahara.

CHAPTER 2

Chills 'n' Thrills

Bwap! The snowball hit me in the back and slid down my T-shirt, leaving an icy wet trail I felt but couldn't see. I spun around, scooped some snow off the ground, packed it into a ball and threw it at Armin. Thunk! Bull's-eye!

We were high in the Atlas Mountains on our way south to the desert, having – that's right! – a snowball fight. That's one of the incredible things about the country of Morocco – in the space of just one day's travel across it, you can swim in the ocean,

We've left Fez...
The city still looks and feels as it must have almost a thous... years ago. Really easy to get lost.

Fez

ATLAS MOUNTAINS

Here Armin and I crossed over the mountains ar... had a snowball fight, on the way down to the desert.

Ksar es Souk

MOROCCO

Merzouga

We're getting near the desert! Orange sand covered part of the road here.

We camped out here on the flat desert after hearing a 'flying saucer'! The thousands of brilliant stars were incredible in the cold night sky.

The desert is sometimes called "an ocean of sand", and it's easy to tell why when you look at the ripples on this sand dune. The only time I had ever seen sand this colour was on a beach.

have a snowball fight in the mountains, and ride a camel in the desert. In fact, the Atlas Mountains are where people from as far away as Europe come to enjoy the snow and go skiing in Africa!

After we left the mountains, I spotted something I had only ever seen on a beach, by the ocean: orange sand. The sand's colour reminded me of seasoned salt I sprinkled on burgers cooked on my barbecue, back in Toronto. This was the first time in my life I had seen sand that colour drifting across a road, far from any water. I was excited – it meant we were at the edge of the Sahara!

I was dying to see the desert, but Armin reminded me that we had to stop for the

night. Evening was coming and it was time to set up camp by the side of the road. I was disappointed. Like it or not, I would have to wait until morning to really see the Sahara. Already it was too dark to see much. But the night sky – that was a different story!

I couldn't get over how many stars I saw above me. There were far more than I had ever seen in Canada and they were bright all the way down to the horizon. For some reason, looking at the night sky made me feel very small and insignificant and very alone. I really felt that I was in another part of the world and far away from all the things that were familiar to me. And I loved it!

As I stood shivering in the cool evening

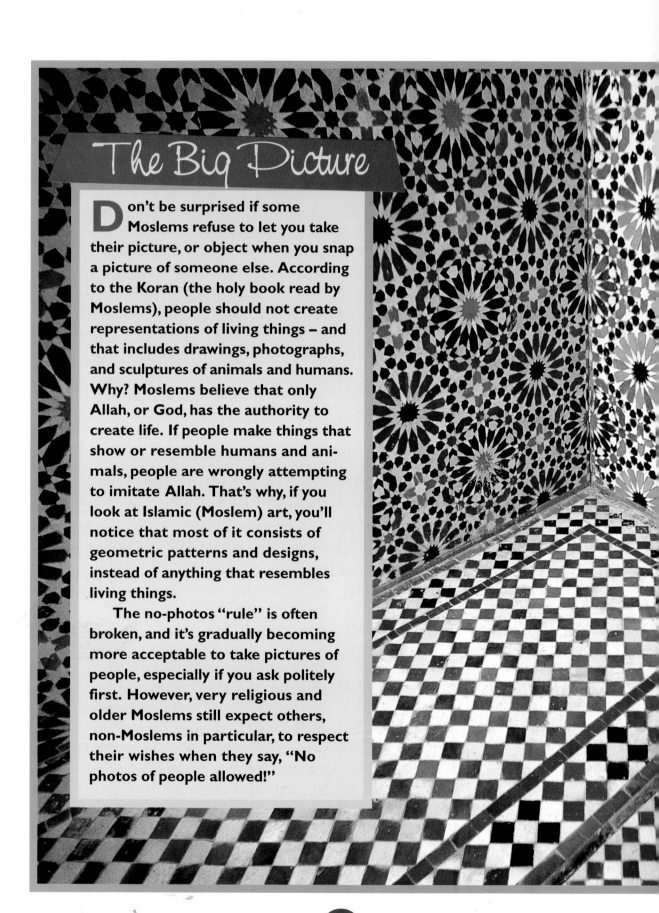

The Big Picture

Don't be surprised if some Moslems refuse to let you take their picture, or object when you snap a picture of someone else. According to the Koran (the holy book read by Moslems), people should not create representations of living things – and that includes drawings, photographs, and sculptures of animals and humans. Why? Moslems believe that only Allah, or God, has the authority to create life. If people make things that show or resemble humans and animals, people are wrongly attempting to imitate Allah. That's why, if you look at Islamic (Moslem) art, you'll notice that most of it consists of geometric patterns and designs, instead of anything that resembles living things.

The no-photos "rule" is often broken, and it's gradually becoming more acceptable to take pictures of people, especially if you ask politely first. However, very religious and older Moslems still expect others, non-Moslems in particular, to respect their wishes when they say, "No photos of people allowed!"

This girl let me photograph her and her photo.

air, I also heard an eerie, high-pitched, very unfamiliar noise. I half expected to see a flying saucer come down out of the sky and land near me – that was what the strange sound made me think of. But that couldn't be…or could it? When I walked over to the telephone poles by the side of the road, I finally discovered the source of the sound. The sudden drop in temperature had caused the telephone wires to shrink, vibrate at a high pitch, and "sing" for a while. So much for flying saucers in the middle of Morocco!

I was so cold that my teeth chattered, so I climbed into my sleeping bag and burrowed deep down for warmth. Already the desert seemed to be very different from what I had expected to find.

What else would I discover tomorrow?

I'll never forget my first desert sandstorm. The wind hit with a fury, the sun vanished, and the temperature plunged. A howling and scraping sound blasted my ears.

CHAPTER 3

What a Blast!

At last! We were in the desert I had dreamed of seeing all these years. But I didn't have much time to run my fingers through the sand or walk in the dunes – a sandstorm was heading our way!

Our first day in the desert had started out calm and clear, so I was astonished to see a big yellow cloud stretched low across the sky, gathering in size and speeding silently toward us. It took me a moment to realize that a sandstorm was coming, but when I did, I screamed to Armin and pointed to the cloud. We didn't have a moment to lose!

Together we furiously gathered up everything we'd taken out of the van when we stopped near some date palms, and closed all the windows in the van. Just as we shut the last one, the wind hit with a fury, the sky grew dark, and the temperature plunged. From inside the van, we watched sand streak by, palm trees bend, and the world turn yellow-brown. A great howling and scraping sound blasted our ears.

The most amazing part was still to come. After the storm blew past us, huge drops of rain began to fall. They were the biggest raindrops I had ever seen – they looked like giant, juicy bugs crashing on the windshield! But within an hour, everything was back to normal. The only reminder that a sandstorm and rainstorm had passed through was in the sand. Hours later, it still felt cool and damp on my bare feet.

In the town of Merzouga, near the place

My first visit to a nomad tent. Great. I learned a lot a couscous meal delicious too

Ksar es Souk

MOROCCO

2 days to Timbuktu

Merzouga

HAR

Armin and I sat in the van through a roaring sandstorm on this part of the track.

Merzouga is a friendly little mud village at the foot of huge orangey sand dunes. I finally feel as if I'm real in the desert.

But you can't cross the Sahara here, so we had back north again.

Mohammed was one of the first African kids I really got to know. He was a big fan of Clint Eastwood and loved talking about his movies.

Desert Dangers

You might think that the most dangerous things people face in the desert are the heat and the risk of running out of water. But desert travellers soon learn to dread exactly the opposite things. When the sun sets at night and the temperature suddenly drops, the intense desert cold can feel worse than the daytime heat, especially if you aren't wearing warm clothing, a hat, and gloves. Water can even freeze overnight in a water bottle. Rainstorms in the mountains can race down to the desert, causing sudden floods and leaving people stranded without food and shelter. It is said that more people have been drowned by flash floods in the desert than have died of thirst.

where the sandstorm had occurred, Armin and I met a boy named Mohammed. Mohammed loved talking about Clint Eastwood, so I tried my best to answer his many questions about Clint and the movies he had starred in. But Mohammed did more than chat about Westerns. After listening to me say how much I wanted to see the people of the desert, he arranged for me and Armin to share a meal with some nearby nomads in their tent. Along with seeing the desert, I had always wanted to see inside a nomad's tent. Now it was finally about to happen!

Stepping into the nomads' tent was like entering another world. The tent was made

Get Wind of This!

How powerful can the wind be during a sandstorm? During one Sahara sandstorm, the wind carried red dust as far away as the Swiss Alps and turned its snow-capped mountain peaks pink!

When I stepped into this nomad tent, I entered another world.

of dark goatskin and had a low ceiling. Brightly coloured blankets and carpets hung around the edges. I also noticed a wall of fabric dividing the tent in two. From the other side of this wall came the voices of women and children and the sizzle of a cooking fire. I breathed in a delicious, spicy smell and hoped that it was coming from the meal being prepared for us.

The side of the tent I was on – the men's side – had pillows for sitting or lounging on, and very little else. The only nomads we saw were some boys lurking in the shadows and our host, an old man. He served us mint tea that I'll never forget. It was the sweetest and most syrupy tea I had ever tasted! I knew it was considered an honour for visitors to receive lots of sugar in their tea, so I drank it even though I didn't like it that sweet.

What's left to do after you climb a dune? Get to the bottom of things! These people are racing down on foot – I also saw kids "sledding" downhill on flattened boxes!

I was still learning to speak Arabic so I sometimes found it hard to understand what the old man was saying or reply to his questions. After I told him that I was from Canada, he asked me, "Are there camels in Canada?"

When I told him that no, there weren't any camel herds there, the old man shook his head in disbelief. He must have felt as surprised at my answer as I did at his ques-tion. We both could hardly believe what the other person was saying!

We shared a delicious meal of spicy couscous and drank one last glass of tea before it was time to say our goodbyes to the nomads. As Armin and I walked back to the van, I realized how quickly the evening had passed. Everything about the Sahara – the people, the landscape, the weather – fascinated me and I just had to see more!

It's Teatime

You're out in the desert and feeling thirsty and hot. It's time for some tea – steaming hot tea, that is! Some (but not all) people believe that drinking hot tea causes you to sweat, which helps you cool off. One thing is certain: hot mint tea is so popular here that it's known as Morocco's national drink.

Moroccan mint tea is always made with tea leaves and fresh mint. It's always served in a glass, not in a cup with a handle, so that you can tell just by touching the rim if the tea is too hot to drink. The first sip might surprise you. Africans add lots of sugar, so the tea tastes very sweet and is almost like syrup. Guests are honoured with even more sugar, which is considered a luxury.

A host always serves three glasses to each guest. Sometimes the glasses will be served right after one another and sometimes there may be long periods of time, even hours, between each glass. Once the three glasses have been served, don't expect to be offered any more. According to tradition, the drinking of the third glass marks the end of your visit – and that means it's time for you to go!

A host always puts out one extra glass to show that an unexpected guest is welcome at teatime too.

The Sahara: Nitty Gritty Facts

🌀 The Sahara is the world's largest desert. It's big enough to hold the entire United States!

🌀 Less than one-quarter of the Sahara is sand. The rest of the desert is covered in gravel and rock.

🌀 The Sahara isn't all flat, as you might expect. In some parts, you'll see towering mountains of sand and rock!

🌀 Some scientists believe that parts of the Sahara were lush grasslands long ago. According to these desert experts, the grasslands existed over a million years ago and were filled with rivers and streams that watered the land. It is possible that elephants, rhinoceros, and antelope once roamed here and fish swam in the water!

Desert landscapes are never dull. In many places, you'll find gravel, boulders and even mountains!

These women are walking near Zagora,
where I saw the strange sign to Timbuktu.

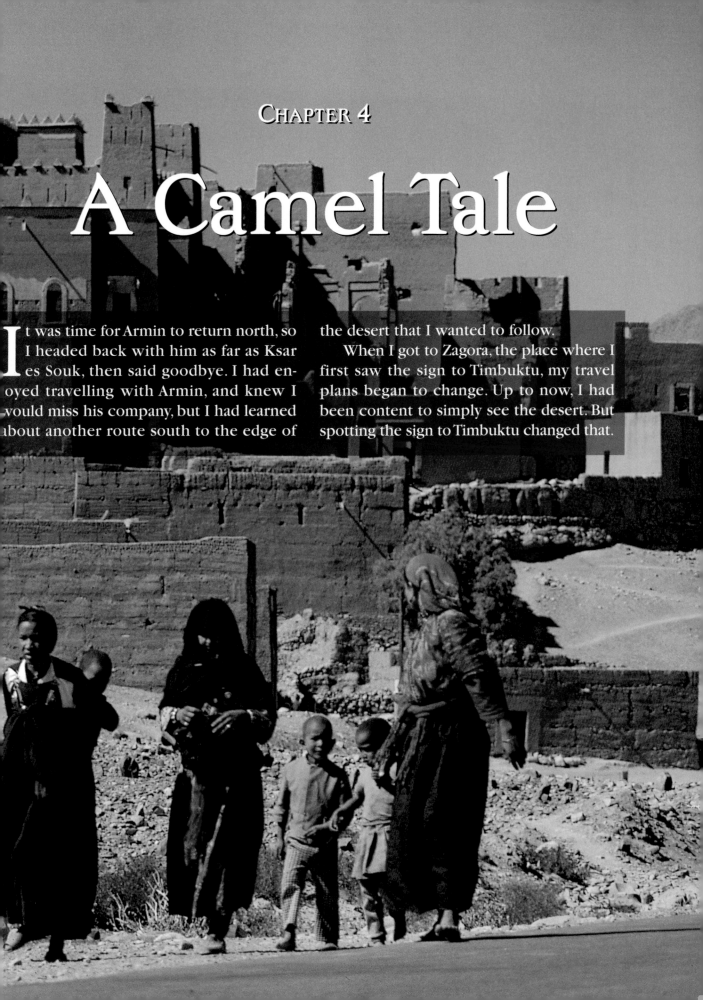

CHAPTER 4

A Camel Tale

It was time for Armin to return north, so I headed back with him as far as Ksar es Souk, then said goodbye. I had enjoyed travelling with Armin, and knew I would miss his company, but I had learned about another route south to the edge of the desert that I wanted to follow.

When I got to Zagora, the place where I first saw the sign to Timbuktu, my travel plans began to change. Up to now, I had been content to simply see the desert. But spotting the sign to Timbuktu changed that.

MOROCCO

ATLAS MOUNTAINS

Ksar es Souk

Marrakesh

52 days to Timbuktu

Merzouga

Zagora

ALGERIA

Mhamid

SAH

You can't cross the Sahara here either, so I went north again, over the mountains to Marrakesh, another ancient caravan destination.

There was a dry salt lake bed called Iriki out here... sort of like where the Space Shuttle lands in Nevada.

Here is where I saw that that fired my imagination and me determined, one way or and to get to Timbuktu!

Here I organized my first camel It was an 8-day circuit with 2 gu named Booba and Boomba. I named my camel Fred.

I always received a great response when I spoke Arabic to people I met on my trip.

Now I wanted to actually go across the Sahara, all the way to Timbuktu. I wasn't exactly sure how I would do that, so in the meantime I decided to keep following the route I was on. I would go to the Sahara's edge one more time before attempting to venture across it.

I was glad that I had decided to do this, because I met a sugar importer in Mhamid who offered to take me and some others on a camel trip. The plan was to take an eight-day journey, by camel, to a dry salt lake in the Sahara. It took some time to plan and organize our trip. We all had to agree on the prices to be paid for the guides and the camels, decide on the provisions we would take

Here are the three most important words you need to know if you meet someone who speaks Arabic:

Bism-Allah ("BEESM-Allah"):
This means "In the name of Allah". This word is spoken before prayers and meals, before entering houses and boarding buses, and before starting anything else new. People who say it are putting their trust in God to make their next actions positive and successful.

Al-hamduli-Allah ("Al-HUM-doo-LEE-Allah"):
This means "Praise be unto Allah". People say this whenever something good happens to them, such as receiving a compliment, eating a delicious meal, or seeing something beautiful. Using this word reminds everyone that all good things come from Allah. Forgetting to use it invites the "Evil Eye" to take away your good fortune.

Insha-Allah ("In-SHA-Allah"):
This means "If Allah wills it" and is said when something in the future is mentioned. For example, "See you tomorrow, insha-Allah." Or "We're coming back to Morocco next year, insha-Allah." Using this word reminds people that only Allah decides and knows what will happen in the future. Forgetting to use this word also invites the "Evil Eye".

I'll Take It!

Many cities and towns throughout Africa hold open-air markets called "souks" (the word rhymes with "dukes"). A souk is the African version of a shopping mall and the perfect place for some one-stop shopping. You'll find almost anything you're in the market for, from fruit and spices to dentists' pliers and dried lizards. And who can pass up the colourful clothing?

with us, and get permission from a local government official, called a khalif, before we could set off. Impatiently I counted down the days until our departure.

The day of the trip, I awoke before dawn to the growling sounds of camels just outside my hotel window. Once the camels were loaded, we led our caravan out of town, just as the sun was rising. When we were past the walls and houses, we climbed onto the camels. The guides, who walked beside us, began singing and chanting to encourage the camels to pick up their pace. Wide awake with excitement, I noticed other sounds that I hadn't ever heard before – the soft, padding sound of the camels' feet, the rhythmic creak-creak of the saddles, and the sloshing of the goatskin water bags that hung on either side of each camel.

Every so often, the camel I was riding (whom I had nicknamed "Fred") would turn his head around and stare disdainfully at me. I didn't like it when Fred did this because camels are cud-chewers and have hideous breath. I soon discovered that a camel's breath is so awful that you can actually smell one coming up from behind before you can see it! Of course, there

That's me in desert clothing, riding Fred and writing about my trip in the journal I always carried. You can see my map roll and my camera bag attached to the back of the saddle. The wobbly movement makes it hard to write or take pictures from a camel's back.

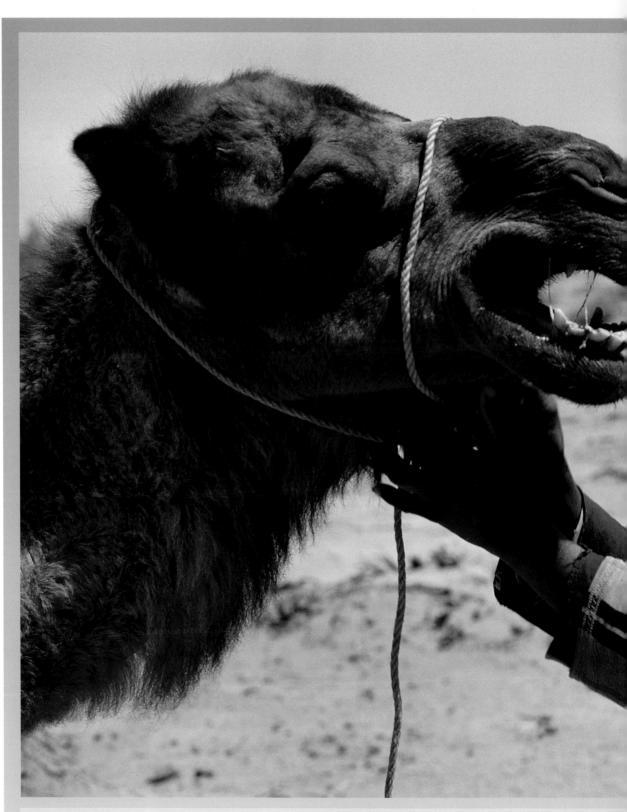

Watch out! If a camel gets angry with you, it might bite or spit and cover you in a sticky mes

I don't know how these boulders got there or why someone built a house so close to them. Talk about a strange Sahara sight!

are far worse fates than having a camel breathe on you – if a camel is really displeased with something you do, it sometimes spits, covering you in a gluey, goopy mess! I hoped that Fred wouldn't try to do that with me!

Each night when it was time to go to bed, we laid out sleeping bags on the sand, first carefully checking for scorpions and poisonous snakes called vipers. I was very wary of scorpions – the first day of our camel trip, I had almost sat on one and narrowly escaped its painful, poisonous sting. But scorpions or not, I loved sleeping under the open desert sky. One of the guides said to me, "It is better to sleep on a stone pillow in the Sahara than to sleep on a soft pillow in a hotel." I wasn't sure if he was serious or not, but I had to agree with him. I had never slept so soundly in all my life!

On the last evening of our trip, as we sat around the fire, a guide pointed to the North Star. "If you're in Timbuktu and want to travel here to Mhamid," he told me, "I've heard that you must follow this star across the desert." Timbuktu! There was that name

How to Climb onto a Camel

If you stand beside a camel that's kneeling on the ground, you'll find out just how big this animal is. Even when a camel is on its knees, its hump comes up as high as a kid. So how do you climb into the saddle on top of a camel's hump? The trick is to plan your moves ahead of time and act fast!

While the camel is kneeling, stand on its left front folded leg. (Don't worry, this doesn't hurt the camel!) Then, grab the far side of the saddle and leap onto it before the camel stands up. (This is where you must be quick, because the camel starts to get up as soon as you step off its leg.) Hang on tight – as the camel stands up, it throws you backward, then forward, and the saddle shifts around, even though it's tied down. Sometimes the camel does a little dance to shake the saddle into place and get it settled comfortably on its hump.

Once the quaking has stopped – and if you're still in the saddle! – it's time to relax and take in the view ahead. Perched high on the top of the hump, you can't see much of your camel except its big head far down in front. It almost feels as if you're suspended in space!

When you walk beside a camel, you spend lots of time looking at camel footprints in the sand (see above). The view from the top of a camel is different. Climbing up takes some fast moves and fancy footwork (see left).

again! Hearing it reminded me that I still wanted to cross the Sahara and see Timbuktu. I had gone as far south as I could on this particular route. Deadly land mines in the sand, left over from past desert wars, made the part of the Sahara south of here very unsafe. As well, there were fiercely protected borders beyond here that were difficult or impossible to cross. I decided to head back north to Marrakesh. I was about to begin the greatest part of my desert adventure.

Mmmmm! Mouth-Watering Bread

Take dough, rocks, sand, and what have you got? The makings for delicious-tasting bread, Sahara-style! Here's how a nomad prepares bread every day while out in this part of the desert.

First, he makes a fire on a bed of rocks, and lets it burn right down. After he whisks away the ashes, he dumps the raw dough directly on the blazing hot rocks.

When the bottom of the bread is s he makes another fire beside the b or waves burning branches over it.

When the bread is done, he whacks it with a stick to remove any grains of sand.

nce the top is seared, the omad uses his turban to our sand on the bread. hen he starts yet another re, on top of the sand, to ake an "oven" for baking e desert bread.

The bread is served hot with a dip called "dwaz", made from water, vegetables, and spices. People who eat desert bread all agree: it tastes much better than "regular" oven-baked bread!

You Can't Top a Turban!

Twist up a long, thin cloth scarf, put it on your head, and ta-da! You've made a turban, the most popular head covering in the Sahara. But a turban is more than a cool hot-weather "hat". Here are ten more ways to use a turban while out in the desert . . .

- untwist it, wet it, then hold it in front of your hot face so the wind comes through it and acts as an air conditioner

- roll it up and use it as a pillow

- twist it and use it as a rope to lower and raise a bucket of water from a well

- tie it tightly around the legs of a camel to keep the camel from wandering too far away

- cover your eyes, nose, and ears with it to block out dust and sand

- towel yourself with it when you're wet

- stretch it out, holding the corners with your hands and feet, to fan a fire

- pour water or camel's milk through it to filter out hair, sand, silt, or algae as you drink the liquid

- tie it into a sling for a broken arm

- wrap things up in it and use it as a temporary "pocket" or sack

A turban makes a great rope for pulling a bucket from a well.

A wet turban dries quickly when you hold it in the wind.

Life isn't always lonely for nomads. Once a year they gather to buy goods, race camels, and have some fun.

CHAPTER 5

Fun in the Sun

I was standing in the main square of Marrakesh, a place known as "the Assembly of the Dead". The square's spooky name dated back centuries, to the time of a certain sultan. You could say he had found a unique way to "head off" problems - to make sure that his subjects obeyed him, the sultan beheaded anyone who rebelled, then stuck their heads on poles around the

Where Am I Now?

This bustling city is all painted pink, with snake charmers and outdoor dentists in the main square.

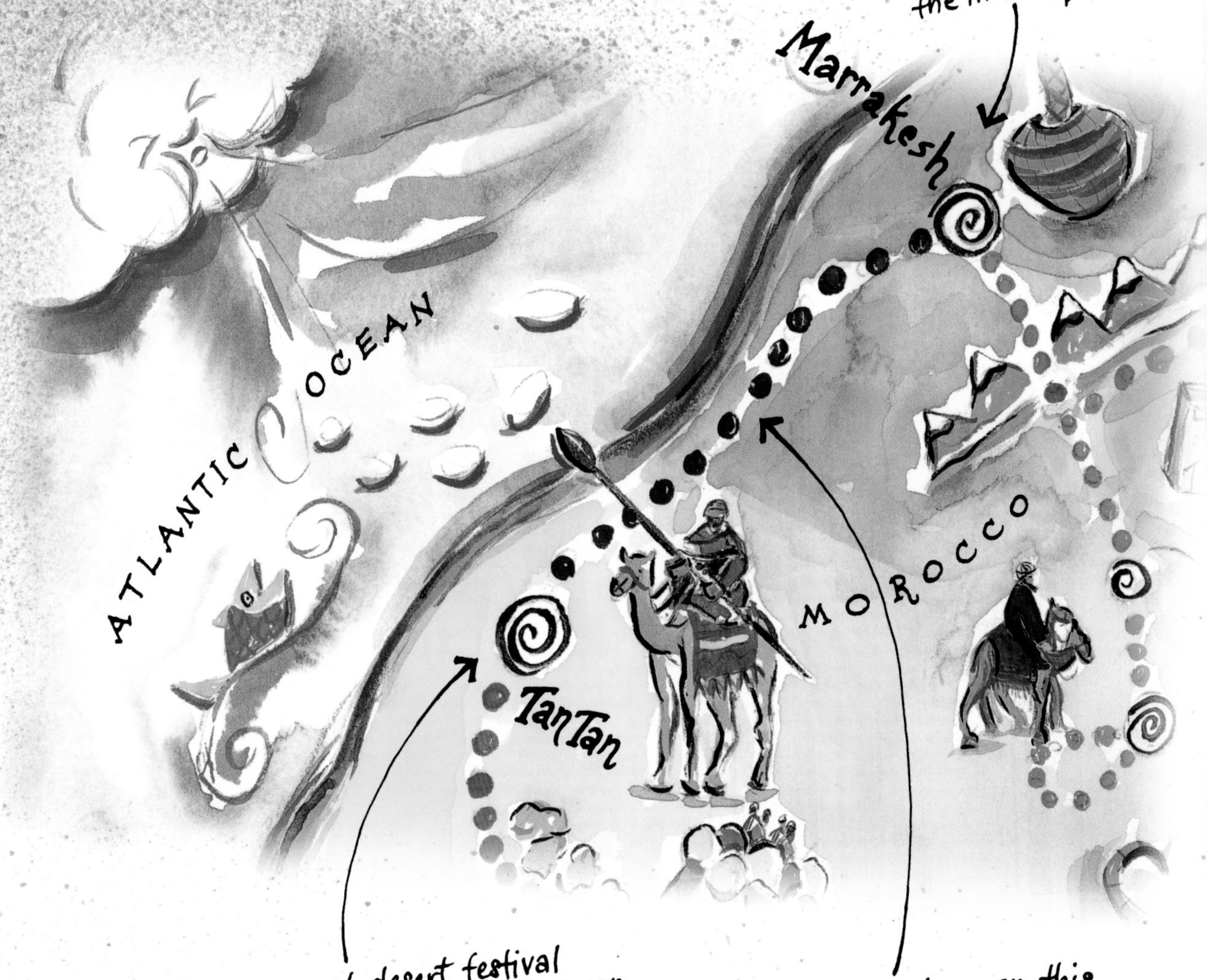

Marrakesh

ATLANTIC OCEAN

MOROCCO

TanTan

A huge annual desert festival was taking place here for tribesmen from all over the western Sahara: hundreds of tents, thousands of camels, music, gossip, trading. And camel races too.

Somewhere on this rickety bus trip, goat pee from the roof splashed in the window all over me!

To show what a popular dentist he is, this man displays all the teeth he has pulled.

square. He did this to remind all of his subjects who was the boss.

Right now, though, there were no signs of dead heads. Instead I felt like I'd been dropped in the middle of a gigantic, noisy carnival, filled with snake charmers and fortune tellers, acrobats and snack sellers, musicians and storytellers. My all-time favourite "entertainer" was a dentist who pulled teeth in the middle of the square. Other people must have liked him as much as I did, because every time the dentist started to pull someone's teeth, a huge crowd gathered around him.

I had wanted to go to Marrakesh for the same reason I had wanted to see Fez. Both cities had once been important destinations along the old caravan routes and are still considered the great cities of Morocco. Marrakesh was a more fun-loving city than Fez, and I was tempted to stay here a while. But I couldn't shake the thought of seeing Timbuktu, so I soon headed south again.

From Marrakesh, I travelled by bus to Tan Tan. Unlike the buses I was used to back home, the buses here overflowed with people, parcels, and even animals. I discovered just how packed a bus could get the day I had my arm out the window and felt

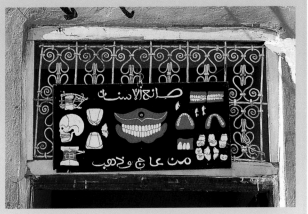

Some dentists have signs like these ones so people with tooth trouble can find them in a hurry.

The Recycle Cycle

Some African people, especially those who are poor, are among the world's best recyclers. They can't afford to buy many new goods, so they'll often take things that have been discarded or become broken or worn out, and put them to another use. Take a look at these photos. Can you spot the objects that have been recycled and tell what they have been turned into?

See bottom of page for answers

Answers: 1. truck axle turned into a merry-go-round 2. half a car transformed into a donkey-powered vehicle 3. tires shaped into water jugs 4. suitcase handle used as a door handle 5. cut-up oil drums made into a fence

And they're off! Over short distances, camels can travel as fast as cars driving along a city street.

some drops falling on it. I looked out, expecting to see a rain cloud, but instead came eye-to-eye with a live goat tied to the luggage rack on the roof, next to some boxes and crates. It was chewing its cud and peeing down the side of the bus at the same time!

I arrived in the town of Tan Tan just in time for the annual "moggar", or desert reunion, also known as "the Great Fair of the Blue Men." It's held outside the town on a huge plain the size of many, many football fields put together. The plain is ringed with hundreds of tents and it's the place where, once a year, thousands of nomads gather and leave behind their solitary way of life. At the moggar they buy goods (everything from fruits and vegetables to digital watches and radios), exchange gossip, buy and sell camels, race camels, and cut loose – sort of like the nomad version of "Spring Break".

Mostly nomads from the south come to this moggar, so for the first time since I'd arrived in Africa I didn't hear much talk about Fez or Marrakesh or Morocco. Instead, everyone was speaking about places to the south: Mali, Mauritania, and Timbuktu.

Timbuktu still seemed unreal to me, but hearing its name encouraged and excited me. It was only a matter of time before I would be able to see it for myself!

Who Are the "Blue Men"?

In many places in Africa, especially in the north, you'll hear people talking about the famous "Blue Men". Take one look at the Blue Men's long, billowing robes and tall turbans and you'll know right away where their colourful name comes from. The Blue Men's clothing is saturated with so much natural indigo dye that the fabric glistens when it's new. Unlike some other dyes, this dye isn't "fixed", or treated to keep it from coming off the fabric. Blue Men can actually turn blue after touching their robes or adjusting their turbans – the dye comes off on their hands and faces, staining their skin the same shade as their robes and turbans.

It's easy to see where the Blue Men's colourful name comes from.

Some Blue Men are nomads known as "Tuaregs". Centuries ago, Tuareg tribes controlled much of the caravan trade across the Sahara, carrying slaves, gold, ostrich feathers, and spices by camel from south of the desert and trading them in the north. Tuaregs still run camel caravans across the last route left in the African desert. On this route, which covers the distance between the salt mines of Taoudenni and the city of Timbuktu, Tuaregs carry salt by camel caravan, just as they have done for centuries.

Other Tuaregs are less fortunate. Once known as proud, noble tribesmen who looked after large herds of goats and camels, today's Tuaregs struggle for survival. Their herds have been diminished due to years of drought, and many Tuaregs have given up their traditional life as nomads to live near the cities, searching for work and trying to adapt to modern ways.

The huge tents the **Blue Men** live in are just as eye-catching as the billowing robes they wear.

Strike a Bargain!

You've gone to an African market and have just spotted something you'd like to buy. But wait a minute – you can't find a price tag. In fact, it's hard to find price tags anywhere in the market. Welcome to a different way of buying and selling goods, where paying for your purchase is the least interesting part, but deciding on the price (or "bargaining") is all the fun! Bargaining is common in many parts of the world. Here's how it usually works . . .

Price tags? You won't find any in this shop.

◎ The shopkeeper tells you the price of the item you're interested in buying.

◎ You offer him half (or less) of that price.

◎ The shopkeeper suggests another price that is lower than his original price, but higher than the one you've just offered. He watches your reaction – this tells him how serious you are about buying the item.

◎ You suggest another amount that is higher than your previous offer, but lower than the price he's just proposed.

◎ You and the shopkeeper continue exchanging prices until you find one that you both agree is acceptable. If you don't like any of the prices that the shopkeeper is offering, you can walk away and hope that he will call you back with a better offer. (The shopkeeper can also stop bargaining if he doesn't like the final price you suggest.) Or you can return the following day and continue bargaining. But don't be surprised if the bargaining starts at a higher price than the one at which you left off!

Unlike making a quick purchase at the mall, bargaining at the market is something that can't be rushed and it does take effort. But bargaining does have one benefit that "regular" shopping doesn't. By the time you're ready to pay for your purchase, the person selling it may seem very familiar, almost like a friend – and that's probably not the way you feel about the salesperson ringing in your purchase at the mall!

Want to
buy a pot or
two? Then
take a deep
breath –
it's time to
find the
shopkeeper
and start
bargaining!

I had never seen these weird, glowing lights
in the Sahara before. When I got closer, I
discovered what they were – bonfires! Travellers
were having "beach parties" on the sand!

CHAPTER 6

Midnight Madness

I leaned forward in the passenger seat of the truck and peered through the windshield, trying to see beyond the small pool of light made by the truck's headlights. Disappointed, I settled back in my seat – it was too dark. We were crossing part of the Sahara at night and I could hardly see anything! I wondered what was out there…

A night-crossing of the desert hadn't been part of my original plans, but when another truck I had hoped to ride in was delayed in Bir Moghrein, I had no choice but to find another ride. That's how I had ended up here, with some other passengers in "the Vulture of the Desert", a big Mercedes truck with its name proudly painted on the front.

Where Am I Now?

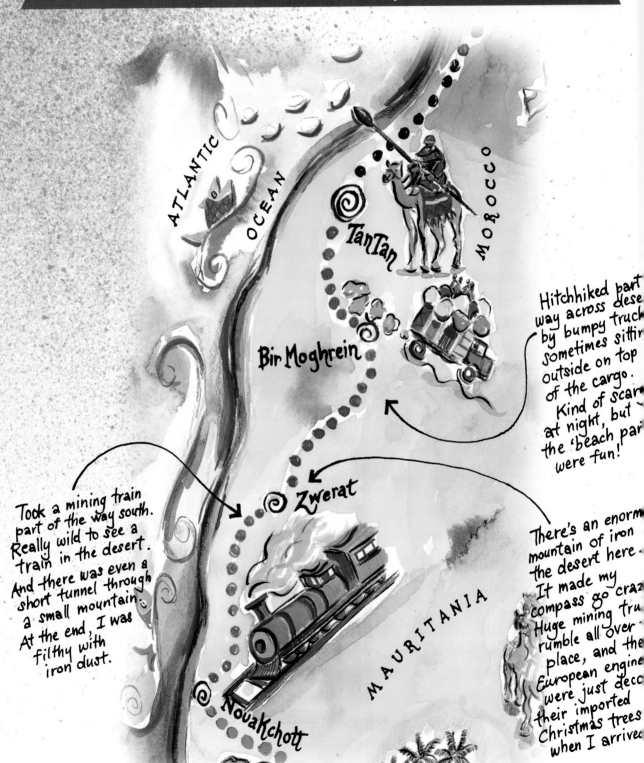

ATLANTIC

OCEAN

TanTan

MOROCCO

Bir Moghrein

Zwerat

MAURITANIA

Novakchott

Hitchhiked part
way across dese
by bumpy truck
sometimes sittir
outside on top
of the cargo.
Kind of scar
at night, but
the 'beach par
were fun!

Took a mining train
part of the way south.
Really wild to see a
train in the desert.
And there was even a
short tunnel through
a small mountain.
At the end, I was
filthy with
iron dust.

There's an enorm
mountain of iron
the desert here.
It made my
compass go craz
Huge mining tru
rumble all over
place, and the
European engine
were just deco
their imported
Christmas trees
when I arrive

See the long "sand ladder" on this truck? It's just the thing to use if you're stuck in soft sand.

Soon, up ahead on the horizon, I did spot something – weird orange glows of light. I was really curious about what they were, especially when The Vulture headed straight toward one of them.

As we drew closer, the glow came into focus as a bonfire. We stopped next to some other trucks, jumped down, and joined the people already gathered around the fire. They were making food, drinking tea, laughing, and calling out to us over the noise of a blaring radio. It seems that we had come across a sort of beach party in the middle of the Sahara! That seemed strange enough, but even stranger was the sight of those other orange glows off in the distance. There were many "beach parties" going on around us!

The orange glows reminded me of ships off in the distance and I thought about something one of the passengers in The Vulture had told me. Apparently, when the French first came to the Sahara, they built lighthouses so that people travelling at night could find their way across the desert. These desert lighthouses even looked like typical lighthouses, with beacons of light that could be seen from far away. The only difference between desert lighthouses and "regular" ones was that the beacons of the desert lighthouses shone over the sand instead of the water.

After we warmed ourselves by the fire, ate some food and had some tea, we said goodbye to the others at the "party", climbed

What's so special about this ordinary-looking building? According to the French words on the wall, this is where you'll find "the not expensive restaurant and modern cleaners"!

back in the truck and rode on to Zwerat. Arriving in Zwerat was like coming into a port. The bright lights from the city looked like the kind you would see at a dock or a harbour. Beach parties, lighthouses, ports – it seemed that everything this night was by the ocean, rather than in the desert.

One of the things I discovered about Zwerat was that it has an enormous mountain of iron. There's so much iron here that a compass is useless when you get close to the town. Instead of always pointing north,

the needle points in the direction of the giant iron mountain!

The Vulture was only going as far as Zwerat, so I boarded a long train loaded with iron ore from the mountain and continued on my way south. I rode in the only passenger car, at the end of the train. Everything in the car, including me, was soon covered in black dust blown back from the cars filled with ore. But I didn't care – I was heading to Timbuktu and that was all that really mattered to me!

What's a Mirage?

The place: the Sahara. The time: day. It's scorching hot, and you're daydreaming about how nice it would be to take a cool, refreshing swim. Suddenly, way off on the horizon, you spot some shimmery, blue water. But don't even think about plunging in – you're looking at an optical illusion known as a mirage!

It may be hard to believe, but the "water" you think you see is actually blue sky. Light rays bend as they pass through the layers of hot and cool air in the desert, and this creates a giant mirror that reflects the sky downward. As you look at the sky's reflection, you notice that it isn't completely in focus. The water looks shimmery, just like a real lake or ocean, due to different pockets of hotter and cooler air, which bend the light waves differently.

What a change from the desert! People wash goats, clothes, even cars in the Niger River.

CHAPTER 7

Almost There...

Mmmmmm! I inhaled the delicious, familiar smell again – what was it? As I stood in the market at Nouakchott and sniffed the air once more, it came to me – I was smelling peanut butter! In fact, now that I took a closer look, I could see that peanut butter was for sale everywhere – marbled peanut butter, chocolate peanut butter, peanut butter by the barrel, even fist-sized, gumdrop-shaped globs of peanut butter

Where Am I Now?

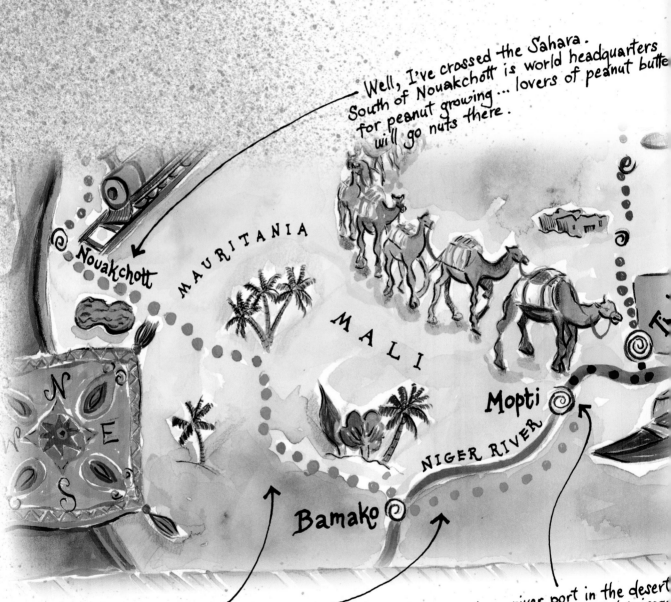

Well, I've crossed the Sahara.
South of Nouakchott is world headquarters
for peanut growing... lovers of peanut butte
will go nuts there.

MAURITANIA

MALI

Nouakchott

Mopti

NIGER RIVER

Bamako

N E S W

South of the Sahara
it's suddenly much greener again.
It's not the jungle yet, but I saw
ostriches and longhorn cattle,
and laughing hyenas startled me
one night near my campsite.
In the river there was even
an old hippo.

A busy river port in the desert
with jumbo canoes called 'piroge
The women wear colourful robes
huge gold earrings. Here I sa
salt bars which had come fi
beyond Timbuktu, and
here I met Tony.

I watched as slabs of salt were unloaded from the boats at Mopti. The salt had just finished an amazing journey. It had been carried by camel to Timbuktu, then shipped here by boat.

that were wrapped up and sold as treats – and all of it was made from peanuts grown nearby. That's one of the things I'll never forget about the capital of Mauritania – the overpowering aroma of peanut butter!

By the time I departed from Nouakchott and arrived in Bamako, the capital of Mali, I had left the desert behind. Instead of sandy areas, I now saw many trees and shrubs. I spotted some hyenas and a wild ostrich by the side of the road. I heard tropical-sounding birds. As the landscape changed, so did the kinds of foods that were available. In North Africa, goats and sheep are raised for food because they're relatively small animals and don't need much water or grass. Here in the

south, where it's greener, I saw herds of cattle and ate steaks instead of goat or lamb shish-kebobs. All these changes excited me – I was getting closer to Timbuktu!

In Mopti, a port on the Niger River, I walked down to the docks to see large slabs of salt being unloaded from the boats. I was told how the slabs had just finished an amaz-ing journey. They had been carved out of the desert salt mines at Taoudenni, carried down by camel to Timbuktu, loaded onto boats, and sent down the river to Mopti. From Mopti, the salt would go to West Africa, which is salt poor and craves the Taoudenni salt.

I had read about the salt slabs and seen photos of them, but nothing compared to

Here's what I saw while travelling along the Niger River. To drive the boat forward, the men thrust their long poles into the riverbed, then walk down the boat as they push on the poles.

seeing them for myself – especially when I remembered that they had been travelling the same way for almost a thousand years!

As I looked at the people washing clothes and cars in the river, and building boats by the shore, I thought some more about those slabs of salt and where they had come from. From the books I had read, I knew that the caravan route from Taoudenni to Timbuktu, a 16-day journey by camel, was one of the last great caravan routes in the world. It was the only major route left in Africa that crossed the desert. Many people thought that the route would probably not be used much longer.

For centuries, people have valued the salt

from Taoudenni because it was believed to have medical and magical powers, but this is changing. Now people are coming with cheaper, easier, more modern ways to get salt from other places. Someday, the caravans carrying their precious cargo of salt from Taoudenni could disappear forever.

Suddenly it seemed that it wouldn't be enough to just go to Timbuktu, important as that still was to me. Seeing those salt slabs really made me want to go beyond Timbuktu, all the way to Taoudenni along the caravan route. How could I get there?

Then came another chance meeting, the kind that travellers sometimes experience in

The Story behind Salt

You might know salt as something you simply sprinkle on food to add flavour. But salt is much more than a tasty mineral. It also preserves food and is something everyone needs to stay healthy. For thousands of years, all over the world, salt has played an important role in people's lives . . .

⦾ Because people couldn't survive without salt and it wasn't always easy to find, salt was thought to be magical and have special powers. In Central and South America, the ancient Aztecs worshipped a goddess of salt. In Japan, it was once customary to sprinkle salt across theatre stages to prevent evil spirits from bewitching the actors. In many places, salt was given to newly married people for good luck.

⦾ Salt was so rare and so highly prized that it sometimes caused wars and invasions. According to salt experts one reason Julius Caesar and the ancient Romans invaded Britain was to find new sources of salt for the Roman people. Salt was also responsible for revolutions and rebellions. One of the causes of the French Revolution was a heavy tax that the King of France placed on salt. Many people who needed salt but couldn't afford to pay the tax rebelled against the royal rulers and overthrew them.

⦾ Some of the world's first roads were built so that people could move salt easily from one place to another. One of the oldest roads in Italy is the Via Salaria. Its name means – you guessed it! – the Salt Route.

⦾ Salt was sometimes used as money. At one time, Roman soldiers were paid part of their wages in salt. This was called a "salarium", and from it comes the modern-day word "salary". In ancient China, the only thing more valuable than salt was gold, and in Timbuktu, salt was considered even more precious. There, it was said, gold and salt had equal value.

faraway places. I was walking back from the docks when I bumped into one of the last people in the world I expected to see – an old friend and fellow traveller named Tony. I could hardly believe my eyes, but there he was!

After we exchanged excited greetings and sat down to share a meal, I blurted out my idea of going to Taoudenni. It turned out that Tony, like me, was heading for Timbuktu. "Let's do it!" he said, after I had finished describing everything I knew about the caravans and their ancient route. "We'll go to Timbuktu, then figure out how to get to Taoudenni. I'll bet we can do it!"

they young or old?
or bold? You can't tell.

ll African women
overed up. In Mali,
this woman (left),
wore her family's
ne on her ears.

In public places, such as streets and restaurants, there are often far more men than women around. Sometimes it's even hard to spot women. The women you do see are often completely covered, with veils over their faces. Only their eyes, hands, and feet show, and there is as much "makeup" on their hands and feet as on their eyes!

According to tradition, men here have a powerful sense of personal and family honour and feel very protective of the women in their family. Men haven't wanted other men to see their wives, so women have spent most of their lives in courtyard homes which were designed so that strangers couldn't see in. In some places, those traditions continue to this day.

There are other differences in the way women are treated that may seem odd to people who don't live here. If you ask a man how many kids he has, he may give you the number of sons he has and not include his daughters, if he has any. Why? Traditionally, girls have been considered less important than boys. A father preferred to have sons, not daughters, so that there would be lots of manpower to help the family cope and survive, especially if life was hard.

In spite of these differences, women also enjoy a warm, secure, and loving family life, with a strong feeling of togetherness. And traditions are changing very quickly in the Arab world. Today, women have more education and legal rights than they ever did before. In some modern areas, such as Casablanca, they have just about as much freedom as women in other parts of the world.

**Was it just another town or a strange,
secret place? I was about to find out . . .**

CHAPTER 8

Timbuktu at Last

The large, flat boat bumped gently against the dock. Our ride from Mopti on the big, brown river was over. We were finally in Timbuktu! I stepped out of the boat and looked around for the city I'd heard so much about.

To my surprise, I couldn't see many buildings, just the river Tony and I had travelled on and a beat-up taxi parked by the docks. The taxi driver took our knapsacks and bags from us and led us to his car. As we drove off, he explained that the city of Timbuktu is several kilometres away from the Niger river. Long ago, the city had been located next to the river, but over time the river had gradually changed its

course and moved away from Timbuktu. When I asked the driver how the salt gets from the city (where the caravan has always made its final stop) to the river docks he told me, "Drivers like me, we carry the salt in our taxis." I was amazed. Between its traditional journey by camel across the desert for 16 days and by boat down the river for about four days, the salt also travels by modern means – in a taxi, for about 10 minutes!

The sun had just set as we pulled in to Timbuktu. Eagerly I looked out the taxi's windows, trying to make out the buildings around us before darkness covered everything. As the headlights shone through the

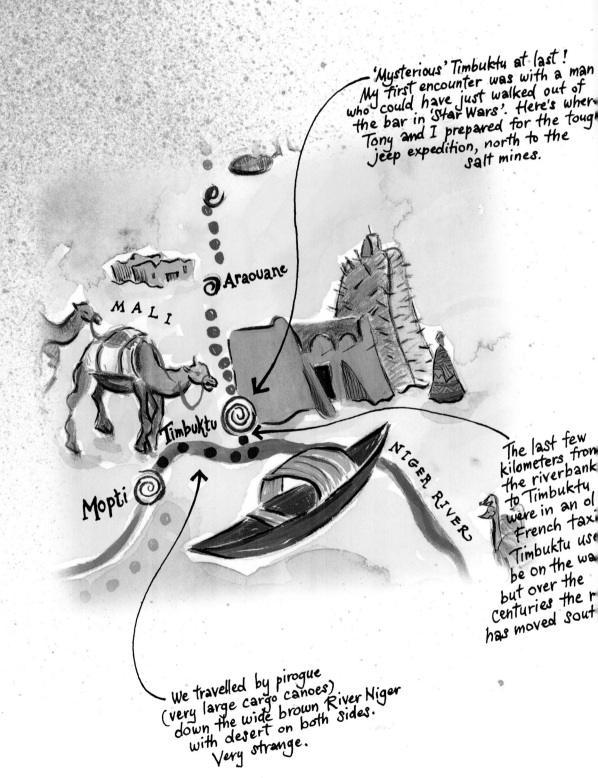

'Mysterious' Timbuktu at last! My first encounter was with a man who could have just walked out of the bar in 'Star Wars'. Here's wher Tony and I prepared for the toug jeep expedition, north to the salt mines.

Araouane

MALI

Timbuktu

Mopti

NIGER RIVER

The last few kilometers fron the riverbank to Timbuktu were in an ol French taxi Timbuktu use be on the wa but over the centuries the r has moved sout

We travelled by pirogue (very large cargo canoes) down the wide brown River Niger with desert on both sides. Very strange.

We arrived in Timbuktu at night. The first thing we noticed was that the streets were soft sand.

dust thrown up from the sand road we were on, everything appeared foggy and vague. The soft, unpaved road also muffled the sounds of our taxi and the occasional person or car we passed. Timbuktu seemed as mysterious as I had always imagined it to be.

Early the next morning, too excited to sleep, I left our small hotel to look around and take pictures. The air felt velvety and cool as I walked up and down the mostly empty streets, looking at low mud and stone buildings and listening to roosters crow.

Suddenly a strange being materialized around a corner. It was tall and thin, and wrapped in black robes and a huge, black turban. A veil covered its mouth and nose and its eyes were metallic sunglasses. As I

gazed up at this creature, I felt as though I were looking at a gigantic, alien ant.

But when it removed its glasses and lowered its veil to speak, I could see that I was face-to-face, not with a bug, but with a man.

"What are you doing?" he asked in French.

"Oh, taking pictures of mysterious Timbuktu," I answered without thinking.

He looked at me quizzically. "Timbuktu is not mysterious," he said. "It is *you* who is mysterious!"

It was my turn to look puzzled. But as I thought about his words, I could see what he meant. For him, Timbuktu was just a familiar, ordinary place where he lived and worked. But outsiders like me – now that was strange!

I soon discovered that Timbuktu didn't look anything like the way it was described in the legends and stories I had read and heard. Centuries ago, Timbuktu had been a thriving caravan city, and a very important place where ostrich plumes, gold, and spices passed through on their way to the rest of Africa and sometimes the rest of the world. At one time, it had been the capital city of a great empire. It had also been a centre of religious learning. People from all over the Moslem world had come to Timbuktu to study at its famous mosque. According to one legend, the city had been so splendid that the roofs of its buildings were made of gold.

But today, there is nothing spectacular about Timbuktu, except the legends. All of the buildings, including its greatest mosque, appeared very ordinary. Some were even decayed or in ruins. A long drought had blackened and killed many of the surrounding trees. Now it's just another small town on the edge of the Sahara.

Yet I wasn't disappointed. After years of hearing about Timbuktu, it didn't matter what it looked like. What did matter was actually being there. When I looked at ordinary objects, like a pop bottle, or did everyday things, like washing my hands, those things became special because of where they were happening – in Timbuktu! And when I pictured a globe and where I was on it, I still could hardly believe it – I had finally made it there. I was in Timbuktu!

There was one more thing that made Timbuktu special for me. It was the place where Tony and I hoped to begin our trip along the caravan route to the salt mines of Taoudenni.

I headed back to the hotel to wake Tony, tell him about the giant ant, and start making our travel arrangements.

I was walking the streets of Timbuktu! That's the main mosque in the background.

What happens if you get lost in the desert? I knew the answer the moment I spotted these sun-bleached camel bones.

CHAPTER 9

In Search of Salt

As the jeep lurched over the dune, I spotted a pile of camel bones, bleached white by the sun. It was the only landmark we had seen since leaving the wells of Bir Ounane, far to the north of Timbuktu. Tony and I were finally on our way to the salt mines of Taoudenni after rounding up fuel, food, water, two jeeps (in case one broke down), spare jeep parts, guides, maps and compasses, and permission from the governor of Timbuktu to go there. Making it as far as Timbuktu had been a big deal for me, but going beyond it, along one of the last caravan routes in Africa, was the ultimate desert adventure. We were heading to one of the remotest places on Earth and I could hardly wait to see it for myself.

This part of the Sahara has been called "a desert within a desert", and it was easy to see why. It's one of the world's hottest, driest areas and there's almost nothing here except earth and sky - no markers, no palm trees,

We made it. These ancient salt mines are the most isolated and remote place in the world's greatest desert!

Here's where I put an old parking ticket on the windshield of Tony's jeep.

Taoudenni

Passed camel bones here! Sort of a warning.

Bir Ounane

North of Timbuktu this is the only village for 1000 miles. It has one tree.

Araouane

M A L I

Timbuktu

Saw our first caravan here. About 50 camels. Later saw many many more, every day, going up and down their 16-day route.

This is the emptiest, most uninhabited place on earth (except maybe Antarctica). Tanezrouft, the local name for this region, means "as naked as the palm of your hand".

From my jeep I saw Tony following my tracks. It felt like we were travelling to the end of the Earth.

not even any litter. Except for the Antarctic, this is the most uninhabited place on the planet. The only people who live on the 500-mile (800-km) route between Timbuktu and Taoudenni are found in the tiny village of Arouane. Out in the middle of nowhere, but close to wells, it looks as though someone had flown in with a giant helicopter and dropped a bunch of houses down onto the sand dunes.

I glanced back at the camel bones and recalled a story our guides had told us about the time, long ago, when 1800 camels and 2000 men died of thirst along this route. We had brought lots of water with us, but if we ever got lost or my jeep became separated from Tony's, the same thing could happen to us. In the desert, the wind covers up tracks very quickly, making it almost impossible to either go back the way you came or search for another vehicle's tracks. It would be easy to end up like those bleached bones, out in the middle of nowhere.

A few hours after leaving Timbuktu we saw an odd sight. On the horizon, and off to the side, a black bubble shimmered in the heat, then vanished. It reappeared, then vanished again. Each time the bubble wobbled into view, it grew bigger. Soon it morphed into a giant centipede inching over the dunes. Finally, when it was closer still, we saw what it really was - a long camel caravan

That's me standing next to a house made of salt. I tasted it to make sure it really was salt!

travelling to the mines. The camels were loaded with supplies for the miners and carried bales of hay to be dropped off along the route for the camels returning south. Tony and I soon lost track of how many camels we saw. We passed thousands of them, going to and from Taoudenni.

Our journey lasted three days, and near the end of our trip I came up with a way to have some fun. The night before we arrived in Taoudenni, I played a practical joke on Tony. I had brought along an unpaid parking ticket I'd received in Toronto, and after Tony went to bed I put it on the windshield of his jeep. I made sure I was watching when he woke up the next morning and looked over at the jeep. The expression on his face was hilarious. Half asleep, he was dismayed to see a parking ticket. Then he remembered where he was!

Later that morning, as we drove over a ridge, I saw a flash of white up ahead. We were coming to the mines! From a distance, I could spot what looked like white, rocky rubble dug up from the salt pits. But when we got closer, I noticed that some of the piles of rubble had tiny windows and open doorways covered by camel skins. I was

This is the pits – and that's no joke! Here's a view of some miners who are working in a salt pit.

Those Incredible Camels!

Camels are so well-suited to life in the Sahara that they are sometimes called "ships of the desert". Here are some uncommon camel facts:

During sandstorms, a camel can shut its nostrils so tightly that blowing sand is blocked out.

A camel can go for days without drinking anything, then guzzle enough water to fill 100 drinking glasses. After a camel quenches its thirst, you can actually hear it "slosh" when it walks!

A camel's hump stores fat, not water, and is a source of energy for the camel. When the camel draws on its supply of fat, its hump changes shape and grows smaller and smaller.

The Camel's Secret Smile

According to one Moslem story, camels always smirk because they know a secret. There are one hundred different names for Allah, or God, but people know just 99 of those names. Only camels know the one hundredth name, and they're not telling.

It's the "Best Smile in the Sahara" Contest. I lost.

You might think that a white camel like this one is a very rare sight in the Sahara. That's not the case – I saw other white camels too. Their colour makes them easy to spot.

Every slab of salt is smoothed and shaped into the same size and weight before leaving the mines.

Rope and straw padding are the only things that hold the salt slabs safely in place on a camel.

looking at the miners' houses, houses that were made of salt.

As we jumped down from the jeeps, I heard the miners calling to each other in Arabic. I listened to the chipping of their tools as they dug for salt. And I couldn't help breathing in a powerful stench, like rotten eggs, that came from the minerals in the water seeping out of the pits. Tony and I had done it – we had made it "beyond the beyond", all the way to Taoudenni. We had come to a place where very few visitors had been for decades.

Taoudenni was filled with everyday things, like men going to work day after day just as people do everywhere. It was also filled with extraordinary things I had never seen before, like houses made of salt, the only building material found here. (Everything else – every tool, every goatskin,

every piece of food – still comes here by camel, as it has for hundreds of years.) But ordinary or not, it was all incredible to me. I had made it to a place so remote that most of the world didn't know it existed. Just being here was amazing – even more amazing than being in Timbuktu!

I soon noticed that only men lived and worked here, because it was felt that the working conditions were too harsh for women. It took two men several weeks to dig down into the ground far enough to reach the salt layer, if they were lucky enough to find it. If they found salt, they would cut a block shape into the surface, and pry out the block. Then the miners would smooth and shape the slab until it had the same weight and measurements as every block before it, going back thousands of years.

I wondered why anyone would want to

Life on a Caravan

What would it be like to work on a caravan? Here are some of the things you would have to do each day:

⊙ walk the entire route on foot beside the camels. Camels in a caravan are usually used to carry supplies and cargo, not passengers. You might walk barefoot or wear sandals made of recycled tires. If you're lucky, you might own softer, leather sandals made of camel skin. Whether your feet are completely bare or covered on the bottom, they are soon covered in callouses, cuts, and blisters.

⊙ gather camel dung and twigs (if you can find them) to use as fuel for the fires. You must do this several times a day. Fires are needed for heating water for tea, cooking food, and also warming everyone at night.

⊙ look after the camels first before taking care of yourself. When you stop at the end of each day, you must unload the camels, hobble them (so they don't wander away), and feed them. After that's all done, you can think about making your own dinner.

⊙ use the sun, stars, and wind to tell where you are and which way to go. For centuries, caravan leaders have been experts at finding their way across the desert without having to count on modern tools such as maps and compasses.

It's Your Move!

Playing checkers in the Sahara is easy to do. First draw a board in the sand with your finger. Then find your playing pieces: twigs on one side and camel dung on the other side!

Taste This!

When you go on a camel trip, it's important to pack foods that don't take up much space, won't go bad in the heat, and don't leak. Here are two popular caravan treats...

◎ "Sahara Bread": Also called "pain du Sahara", this is a clump of dry dates that will keep for up to a year.

◎ Camel's milk: When there are lots of female camels in the caravan, this is the perfect desert drink. There's always a fresh supply on hand! Camel's milk is watery, with a walnut flavour. For a special breakfast treat, it's served hot with sugar.

do this back-breaking work until a worker explained that the miners keep one-quarter of all the slabs they mine – they literally carve their own paycheques. The camel drivers, who take the other three-quarters of the slabs as payment for their services, carry the miners' slabs with them back to Timbuktu and "deposit" those slabs with the miners' families there.

A caravan was about to be loaded with its valuable cargo, so Tony and I wandered over to the loading grounds, off to the side of the pits. We watched as the caravan master selected the best slabs from nearby stacks. Then workers slowly and carefully strapped four or six of the slabs onto each camel, using rope and straw padding to hold them in position. After the last slab was in place, the men tied the noisy camels head-to-tail to form a long chain. The caravan was ready to begin its sixteen-day journey south.

As the caravan set off, Tony and I stood silently as though it were the most important thing in the world. We watched the little plumes of dust that swirled up from the camels' feet and listened as the drivers sang to their beasts. Gradually the caravan grew smaller and smaller as it moved off into the distance. After a long while, it looked like a tiny black bubble. It wobbled in the heat, then vanished, reappeared, then vanished again, fading into a silver mirage that shimmered on the horizon.

We remained there watching until even the mirage disappeared. Still we stood there, straining to hear the camel drivers, until the hot wind erased the last sounds of their singing.

At last we turned away. It was time to prepare for our own long journey home.